"Love Holds No Grievances"
THE ENDING OF ATTACK

"Love Holds No Grievances"
The Ending Of Attack

TARA SINGH

LIFE ACTION PRESS
Los Angeles

First Edition – 1983
Second Edition – 1986
Third Edition – 1988

Library of Congress Cataloging in Publication Data
Singh, Tara, 1919-
Love holds no grievances.
1. Foundation for Inner Peace. Course in miracles
2. New Age Movement.   3. Spiritual Life.   I. Title.
BP605.N48S57 1988 299'.93   88-9341
ISBN 1-55531-226-8 Softcover

10 9 8 7 6 5 4 3

The paper used in this publication
meets the minimum requirements
of American National Standard for Information Sciences –
Permanence of Paper for Printed Library Materials,
ANSI Z39.48-1984.

The material from *A Course In Miracles*
and *The Gifts Of God*
are used by permission of the publisher
and copyright owner,
the Foundation for Inner Peace,
P.O. Box 1104, Glen Ellen, California 95442.
"Love Holds No Greivances" is Lesson 68
of *A Course In Miracles*.

Cover design by David Wise,
Wise Creative Services, Montpelier, Vermont.

I am most grateful for the goodness of the following friends for assisting in the preparation of the third edition of this book: Lucille Frappier, Jim Cheatham, Acacia Williams, Clio Dixon, Frank Nader, and Norah Ryan.

In addition, I am thankful for those instrumental in preparing the earlier editions of this book: Joy Kealey, Nolyn Johnson, Charles Johnson, Sue James, Don Leach, Lara Petiss, Connie Willcuts, Sandra Lewis, Jean Kohn, Kris Heagh, Ted Ward, and John Williams.

Contents

	page
Preface to the Third Edition	9
Preface to the Second Edition	11
Introduction	13

Part I

Chapter One
Clear Direction — 17

Chapter Two
Lesson 68 —
"Love Holds No Grievances." — 25

Chapter Three
The Ending of Attack — 29

Part II

Chapter One
What Is Relationship? — 45

Chapter Two
Healing Relationships — 57

Chapter Three
All Relationships Must End In Love — 71

page

"The Timeless Gifts"   *89*

Addenda

    The Path of Virtue   *93*

    Biography of Tara Singh   *97*

    References   *101*

    Other Materials by Tara Singh
    Related to *A Course In Miracles*   *105*

Preface to the Third Edition

If you explore deeply enough
and recognize the true meaning of
Love holds no grievances,[1]
you will realize that only a saint
can be free of grievances.

It is impossible for the ego
to let go of grievances
in favor of Love.

Man has to see the fallacy
of the very thought system
of relative knowledge
to live by Love that is Absolute
and has no opposite.

To bring a relationship to harmony
demands the undoing
of one's concepts and ideas.
It is the undoing that awakens new potentials
that will not allow you to limit yourself
to your own opinion.

For the wise, the externals are never the issue.
Action always starts
with one's own internal correction.
It is the action of Love,
independent of personality,
that effortlessly transforms relationship.
There are beneficient forces at work in Life.

When God is the strength in which you trust[2]
you are not alone.
The capacity is in each one of us
to outgrow and undo every deception.

A Course In Miracles points out:

> *My grievances*
> *hide the light of the world in me.*[3]

It is this internal light of Love
that shines away the world of illusions.

Tara Singh

Preface to the Second Edition

_____

Love is Absolute;
it is the source of creation.
Love, the Will of God, and Truth are indivisible.
The world of relative thought
will not know the Absolute.

The purpose of the Absolute
is to undo that which is not real.
But who truly aspires to undo
deception, attachments, misperception?

Truth is not generated by ideas.
Only the Silent Mind
has the space to heed beyond littleness.

It is a blessing to accept Love in your life,
to dispel all illusions and not be of the world.
No one can describe this glory
for it has no opposite.
It silences the mind.
But everything we know is of time.

The SELF God created is of Love —
whole and eternal.
By the stillness and the energy of Love
the world is transformed.

Tara Singh

Introduction

A Course In Miracles is not a course of ideas. Ideas are of the physical senses of the body and have no existence in themselves. Being abstract, ideas are part of the thought system of man. We can have ideas without knowing Reality.

A Course In Miracles is independent of the thought system of man. It relates one directly to the fact which dissolves the duality of thought and ends conflict. This conflict-free state is what the Course is about.

Therefore, to read the Course requires a different quality of attention. Attention slows down the process of thought and brings the mind to a quiet state capable of receiving the Given. In that quietness the Course assures us,

There is a message waiting for you . . .[1]

Love holds no grievances.[2]

Part One

Chapter One

Clear Direction

---

*A*t twilight the vibrations of the day change. There is peace upon the land. This is the time when the wise eat a light meal and prepare to sit in quiet and hold hands with God. As night descends upon the planet, they go to bed and experience a different quality of sleep. There is an awakening that takes place before the dawn — the awakening that takes place within man, not just in the world.

> *Love holds no grievances.*
> *I would wake to my Self*
> *By laying all my grievances aside*
> *And wakening in Him.*[1]

Thus they start the day with a clean slate, having no memory of yesterday. They shine bright as the sun with their innocence. Innocence gives space to newness.

Are we ever with the newness? We are so full of our knowings. What a destructive thing it is, this so-called "knowing" that does not know, this thought system of man that perpetuates separation. It is an attack on newness, on Life.

Love holds no grievances is a very important lesson, and I wonder if anyone has paid attention to it in a deep, profound way. What does the lesson mean beyond the words? To go beyond the words we need a clear direction. The Author of *A Course In Miracles* gives this direction saying:

> *I need devoted teachers who share My aim of healing the mind.*[2]

But before we can become the teachers, we have to be the students. And He reassures us, lovingly:

> *I will teach with you and live with you if you will think with me . . .*[3]

Can you think with the Christ? Have you ever really paid attention to this? There is a prayer in the *Text* that reads:

> *I am here only to be truly helpful.*
> *I am here to represent Him Who sent me.*
> *I do not have to worry about what to say or what to do, because He Who sent me*

will direct me.
I am content to be wherever He wishes,
knowing He goes there with me.
I will be healed as I let Him
teach me to heal.[4]

This is a clear direction.

When you have clear direction, you look at things in a different way. Clear direction ends our wandering through experience without purpose. It gives one a kind of passion in which the externals are no longer overwhelming. Passion becomes compassion.

Once your clear direction is *I am here only to be truly helpful,* you have a zest and a passion, do you not? There is an urgency. When your whole mind is moving towards something, you work with life forces. Your intent makes it work and life cooperates.

With *I am here only to be truly helpful* as your single purpose, *Love holds no grievances* will have another meaning. It will become a necessity. If we read it intellectually, without clear direction, do our grievances really end? Direct awareness of a truth is what ends conflict. Therefore, we have a responsibility not to introduce more words. We already "know" too much and apply too little. Words take us away from the intensity of silence and awareness brings us to it. So, our learning is not real if it takes us away from silence. No matter how well we know *Love holds no grievances* intellectually, mere concepts will not work.

If we are learning in order to eliminate words, then grievances end and healing takes place. To be healed and to heal is to rise to another state of being — the actuality of Love rather than descriptions about It.

> *You who were created by Love like Itself can hold no grievances and know your Self. To hold a grievance is to forget who you are.*[5]

Grievances, full of anger and blame, are a preoccupation with the past. Suppose someone says to you that you are a bad person and you feel that it is a wrong accusation. The hurt goes on and on. You cannot stop the emotional and mental process of reaction. But how does the hurt in you, the grudge in you, continue? How do you sustain it?

Somehow we are so self-destructive in our perpetuation of conflict. "He was so mean." "I don't know why she said that to me," and so forth. We can call it hurt; we can call it insult. And indeed, the other person might be mean or insulting. But our own reactions and thoughts are more detrimental than they ever were. They are no longer even around and we go on destroying ourselves by continuing our internal conflict and reaction!

If this can be seen, then a discovery is made. The energy of life is given. Our life is a gift of God to us. We live by that energy — that is what life is, what makes our hearts beat. This energy created the nervous system, the toenails that grow, everything, even the sounds, the vibrations. This is the energy and it is involuntary. We did not invent it. But what use do we make of it? If we make right use of it, we are extending something that is of Heaven; if we do not, we are violating a law which can only lead us to unhappiness, to exploitation of ourselves, our brother and sister.

Love holds no grievances.
Let me not betray my Self.[6]

Are you willing to see that what you call "me and mine" is self-destructive? It separates the "other" and brings isolation upon itself. When you realize this, you will not have any grudge against the world because you have taken care of your own fears and illusions. This means that having come to a totally different perspective, the relationship you have with another is of love. For relationship is love and is free of dependence.

Where there is dependence, there is always friction. Dependence seeks pleasure because it is sad. Can you see that sorrow and pleasure are one and the same?

In relationship there is no expectation, no conflict. It is intrinsic, complete and perfect. It has its own happiness, for happiness is within us and independent of all things external. It has no need to acquire things. It is a joy within, renewing itself all the time. And no circumstances can affect that joy. Your heart is full of gratefulness, for the world of creation is very beautiful. The wise is ever at peace with a heart full of love.

How nature unfolds through morning to night, through the different moods of the day! How it is clothed with the blue skies and clouds! It is a joy to see the hills and mountains, the face of a child — just the perfection of your own hand. It is miraculous.

Where is there the space for hurt? What other people do, let them do. You have the responsibility to find out about your own eternity. Leave other peoples' shortcomings alone. Only in the manmade world is there friction and sorrow.

And this friction and sorrow, the exploitation of man, affect the very crust of the earth that sustains our life. We must change our attitude. Man will not survive without love.

I would see you as my friend,
That I may remember you are part of me
And come to know myself.[7]

Can we really forgive and not preoccupy our minds with the thoughts we hold against others? That cleansing within has to be done by each individual. You are responsible because the mind is the Mind of God. What you put into it, you are responsible for.

The mind that has no reaction in it is absolutely pure and innocent. This is the mind we have to come to before going to bed. The quality of your sleep changes. We place our physical body into His Hands, in sleep for restoration. We must keep our minds free of fear and the dislike of people. Then we will have something to impart that is not of thought, another atmosphere where a human being can grow.

Discover your own holiness. Bring a new order to your life. Put away the newspapers and televisions that influence and stimulate you with stories of hate and murder. Read *A Course In Miracles.* How blessed we are to have three hundred sixty-five lessons, one each day for a year! Give it the space in your life. Read it with reverence. Do not conclude about it. It is too vast. It is too sacred.

Before beginning to read, establish a relationship with it. Come to quiet. Then you will read with a still mind as if you are reading with your heart — not just words. The more grateful you become, the more receptive you become.

Chapter Two
Lesson 68
"Love Holds No Grievances."
(from *A Course In Miracles*)

---

*Y*ou who were created by Love like Itself can hold no grievances and know your Self. To hold a grievance is to forget who you are. To hold a grievance is to see yourself as a body. To hold a grievance is to let the ego rule your mind and to condemn the body to death. Perhaps you do not yet fully realize just what holding grievances does to your mind. It seems to split you off from your Source and make you unlike Him. It makes you believe that He is like what you think you have become, for no one can conceive of his Creator as unlike himself.

Shut off from your Self, Which remains aware of Its likeness to Its Creator, your Self seems to sleep, while the part of your mind that weaves illusions in its sleep appears to be awake. Can all this arise from holding grievances? Oh, yes! For he who holds grievances denies he was created by Love, and his Creator has become fearful to him in his dream of hate. Who can dream of hatred and not fear God?

It is as sure that those who hold grievances will redefine God in their own image, as it is certain that God created them like Himself, and defined them as part of Him. It is as sure that those who hold grievances will suffer guilt, as it is certain that those who forgive will find peace. It is as sure that those who hold grievances will forget who they are, as it is certain that those who forgive will remember.

Would you not be willing to relinquish your grievances if you believed all this were so? Perhaps you do not think you can let your grievances go. That, however, is simply a matter of motivation. Today we will try to find out how you would feel without them. If you succeed even by ever so little, there will never be a problem in motivation ever again.

Begin today's extended practice period by searching your mind for those against whom you hold what you regard as major grievances. Some of these will be quite easy to find. Then think of the seemingly minor grievances you hold against those you like and even think you love. It will quickly become apparent that there is no one against whom you do not cherish grievances of some sort. This has left you alone in all the universe in your perception of yourself.

Determine now to see all these people as friends. Say to them all, thinking of each one in turn as you do so:

> *"I would see you as my friend,*
> *That I may remember you are part of me*
> *And come to know myself."*

Spend the remainder of the practice period trying to think of yourself as completely at peace with everyone and everything, safe in a world that protects you and loves you, and that you love in return. Try to feel safety surrounding you, hovering over you and holding you up. Try to believe, however briefly, that nothing can harm you in any way. At the end of the practice period tell yourself:

> *"Love holds no grievances.*
> *When I let all my grievances go*
> *I will know I am perfectly safe."*

The short practice periods should include a quick application of today's idea in this form, whenever any thought of grievance arises against anyone, physically present or not:

> *"Love holds no grievances.*
> *Let me not betray my Self."*

In addition, repeat the idea several times an hour in this form:

> *"Love holds no grievances.*
> *I would wake to my Self*
> *By laying all my grievances aside*
> *And wakening in Him."*

Chapter Three
The Ending of Attack

---

*My grievances hide
the light of the world in me.*[1]

*W*hat a truth! What a fact! My preoccupation with grievances is a preoccupation with thought that deprives me of knowing love. Yet I begin to see that the light is within. Is there not a delight then, that the light is in me?

Now we need not be sad. If we do not feel it then we are just repeating words. Now you need not be sad. This requires some conviction, but the passion is within you. Do not underestimate yourself. You are holy and what is holy is boundless.

We have to discover the strength of truth. It is truth that liberates man. Freedom has never been known by anyone who has allowed choice to rule him. Choice is born of the fear of consequences. Choice is a deviation from the Will of God.

> *No one can look upon what your grievances conceal. Because your grievances are hiding the light of the world in you, everyone stands in darkness, and you beside him.*[2]

You are in darkness and whoever you are talking to is also in darkness — two projected images talking with one another. We become so artful and poetic in strengthening our images!

Not unless we are contained would we have the energy to dissolve grievances. To be contained means to be responsible not to pass your negativity on to another person. You deal with it without poisoning another. Perhaps you can share with someone very close and dear to you. But make sure they have a mind of their own, a friend who imparts wisdom. Usually we pick someone who can be influenced. We avoid the wise so we can continue our own point of view.

We talk about feelings. But feelings are not permanent. The person about whom you hold your deepest grievances you may have felt good about at one time. So, how can you depend on feelings? They are part of emotion and the body; they change, fluctuate. What you like today, you may dislike tomorrow.

The Course makes it clear that there are but two emotions. One is fear and the other is love. In between is the space where we like to dwell so we can compromise. Feelings are at the realm of duality, so they are not real. Thoreau said, "Serenity is above emotion and expression." Serenity is an intensity that is silent. It has a different vitality. It is contained.

We prefer to remain casual and avoid challenges. But when we are complacent and not consistent with our deeper purpose, there are earthquakes, outside and inside. Life brings crisis. Is that what it takes to wake us up? When you have a challenge, you have to face yourself.

The lesson continues:

> *But as the veil of your grievances is lifted, you are released with him. Share your salvation now with him who stood beside you when you were in hell.*[3]

Can we recognize the hell of our own judgments against others or do you just read the words? If we are not spacious we are reduced to the personality level. The minute we hold grievances or react, we separate ourselves from the vitality of life. Then we only know and live by reactions. Whatever we put into the brain is what we become. If I react to you, I become the reaction. Convinced of it, I isolate myself and deny the light.

> *He is your brother in the light of the world that saves you both.*[4]

Unless we come to that light we will not know how to love the other because we do not love ourselves. Light cannot communicate with a preoccupied mind.

Are you beginning to see how much there is in just one paragraph of the Course? And your reading will improve as you read the next paragraph if you are reading to receive the truth. Your state of being changes with each sentence. Each sentence contains a miracle. And each miracle unfolds into another miracle. You are no longer reading with the same mentality with which you started. You are becoming part of the process of Atonement.

In the *Text*, the Teacher clearly states:

> *I am in charge of the process of Atonement... When you have been restored to the recognition of your original state, you naturally become part of the Atonement yourself.*[5]

By the time you reach the end of the lesson you will be in a different state. Then you have read the lesson. Otherwise it is a ritual.

> *Today let us make another real attempt to reach the light in you. Before we undertake this in our more extended practice period, let us devote several minutes to thinking about what we are trying to do.*[6]

Do you have a few minutes? Usually we do not. We read the lesson from the momentum of our past with its fatigue and routine. We need to come to the real light in us. This is application. Stopping for a moment is to step out of time. And the One Who said, "...*devote several minutes,*" is the One Who is telling us He will live with us if we will think with Him. He is with us when we read *A Course In Miracles* and He will help each one of us to step out of stimulation.

> *We are literally attempting to get in touch with the salvation of the world. We are trying to see past the veil of darkness that keeps it concealed. We are trying to let the veil be lifted, and to see the tears of God's Son disappear in the sunlight.*
>
> *Let us begin our longer practice periods today with the full realization that this is*

so, and with real determination to reach what is dearer to us than all else. Salvation is our only need.[7]

Can you imagine that if salvation is your only need, then everything else is provided? Will you make that your only need? Everything else would be given. Then you would discover that you are afraid and insecure because salvation is not your need.

In each lesson there is a challenge and a miracle. You have to first face the challenge and then the miracle imparts its light. My resistance to the challenge is something that I project and the miracle gives insight. So then there is no challenge at all. I am part of the Will of God. This is what freedom is. This is what it means to lift the veil.

You can not just go on reading; something has happened. You dance in the sky and you come back caressing the stars. You are so boundless. Do you not feel that way? Joyous inside?

Can you remember that salvation is your only need? Just be clear about that, and all the other things that you are giving importance to will fall away. Then you will find you are not of the world. There is gratefulness for the world because it provides everything. Grievances end. Your heart is full of joy.

> *There is no other purpose here, and no other function to fulfill. Learning salvation is our only goal. Let us end the ancient search today by finding the light in us, and holding it up for everyone who searches with us to look upon and rejoice.*[8]

Are you willing to end the conflict of choices and preferences and self-promotion? See the fact that you are in the dark and so is everyone else. If we saw that, free of the words, some other energy comes into being — the energy of awareness. Just the seeing itself is an action. If I am going to "do" something then I project a plan and again get preoccupied with self-centeredness. I have to do nothing about it and allow the seeing to dissolve the darkness. This is the miracle.

> *Very quietly now, with your eyes closed, try to let go of all the content that generally occupies your consciousness.*[9]

You have only to *let go*. This is another state of being, free of words. Where there are no words, there is no choice. There is freedom in silence and innocence.

> *Think of your mind as a vast circle, surrounded by a layer of heavy, dark clouds. You can see only the clouds because you seem to be standing outside the circle and quite apart from It.*
>
> *From where you stand, you can see no reason to believe there is a brilliant light hidden by the clouds. The clouds seem to be the only reality. They seem to be all there is to see. Therefore, you do not attempt to go through them and past them, which is the only way in which you would be really convinced of their lack of substance. We will make this attempt today.*[10]

I am in the dark clouds and that is the only reality I know. Only my self-centeredness, my knowing, and my choices prevent me from going further. Each person has to find out exactly what it is that holds him back. What is your thought system saying to you that keeps you preoccupied? You give energy to preoccupation rather than to going past the clouds. That same energy can be dissipated by thought or, if conserved, used to penetrate the clouds. There is only one energy. Either you waste it with your thoughts or you bring the thought to silence, penetrate the clouds, and see the light that you are.

Every moment you make the choice. The only choice man has ever made is to be separate from God. Now you have seen the futility of choice. Thought always provides you with an alternative, an opposite. When you come to the Will of God there is no more conflict of choices. And everything in the world is yours, the whole universe. What a gift!

> *After you have thought about the importance of what you are trying to do for yourself and the world, try to settle down in perfect stillness, remembering only how much you want to reach the light in you today — now! Determine to go past the clouds. Reach out and touch them in your mind. Brush them aside with your hand; feel them resting on your cheeks and forehead and eyelids as you go through them. Go on; clouds cannot stop you.*

> *If you are doing the exercises properly, you will begin to feel a sense of being lifted up and carried ahead. Your little effort and small determination call on the power of the Universe to help you . . .*[11]

We feel helpless, don't we? We say, "I do not know how to do this." Or, "I cannot do that." Helplessness is the voice of dissipated energy.

The energy of Life is being dissipated by our constant preoccupation with thought. But when we make even a little effort to wake up, everything in the universe comes to help us and we are no longer helpless. The Divine Hand extends the action of Grace, even though we have dissipated our energy and feel helpless. It does not say, "Well, then, you have got to do something! I am not responsible. You have dissipated the energy!" There is no accusation in the Grace of God. The Grace is given; It is ever accessible. The difficulty lies in our receiving It. Discover this as a fact. Truth will introduce you to the vitality of the Universal Forces, the Love of God, and the Action of Grace.

Nobody taught the child to cry. He never went to school to learn it. He cries and the mother responds. So, the minute you feel a real need — the need is a vacuum, a gap — creation fills it. Then there is only joy in your heart, not conceit that you did it. The joy is the discovery of the action of the Will of God. From then on, in that trust, your problems are solved.

He assures us:

> *If it helps you, think of me holding your hand and leading you. And I assure you this will be no idle fantasy.*[12]

But you have to say the prayer in that state of certainty. Then you will discover that helplessness is finished. Salvation has become essential for you! And your prayers have been answered, perhaps not in words, but you will receive the vitality.

> *Your little effort and small determination call on the power of the universe to help you, and God Himself will raise you from darkness into light. You are in accord with His Will. You cannot fail because your will is His.[13]*

Your will is helpless only when it is not consistent with His Will. Never complain about being helpless. You will only complain if your will is not in accord with God's. As long as it is not, you are going to be isolated.

> *Have confidence in your Father today, and be certain that He has heard you and answered you. You may not recognize His answer yet, but you can indeed be sure that it is given you and you will yet receive it. Try, as you attempt to go through the clouds to the light, to hold this confidence in your mind. Try to remember that you are at last joining your will to God's. Try to keep the thought clearly in mind that*

*what you undertake with God must
succeed. Then let the power of God work
in you and through you, that His Will and
yours be done.*[14]

How strong these words are! Your choices are
finished. Your will has become one with the Will
of God.

*In the shorter practice periods, which you
will want to do as often as possible in view
of the importance of today's idea to you
and your happiness, remind yourself that
your grievances are hiding the light of the
world from your awareness. Remind
yourself also that you are not searching for
it alone, and that you do know where to
look for it. Say then:*

*"My grievances hide the light of the world in me.
I cannot see what I have hidden.
Yet I want to let it be revealed to me,
For my salvation
and the salvation of the world."*[15]

How can one have grievances and hurt feelings now that one has the Grace of God? It is
finished.

THE WAY IS SHOWN.

THE PATH IS CLEAR.

AND THERE IS SERVICE.

Part Two

Chapter One
What Is Relationship?

(The following is a dialogue that took place with the father of a young child. Friction entered the family situation with the coming of the child because both parents held different views about the child's upbringing and each one vied for the child's affection.)

*W*e are talking about a family in which there is no real harmony, where the temperaments of the husband and the wife are different. You have a child you love and your wife loves the child as well. But the love of both parents for the child brings about friction. What kind of sense does that make?

The wife wants things her way, you want things in a different way. The child has nothing to do with it. And because each parent cares for the child no one knows what to do.

If we could only see that all the misery in human life is limited to relationship with one another. Why? Because we don't know what relationship is. We have no quarrel with the walls and the birds and the earth; we don't have to forgive the deer. But forgiveness between one another is difficult. We just can't seem to do it. We would rather die or go to so-called hell, but we can't forgive. And so the situation builds up and gets very intense. It doesn't seem to make much sense, does it?

I say that one has to resign. We think we understand what "resign" is, but we don't know the *actuality* of what it is. One could be resigned out of common sense or resigned out of help-lessness: "There is nothing I can do; it is so." Well, I am not talking about either one of these.

The "resign" I am speaking of is the one that starts with, "I don't know what relationship is." At best we know relationship in a certain setting: this is my husband, this is my wife, and this is my child. At best. If we limit relationship to that small frame, it is not complete.

Relationship may go on for lifetimes. Relationship is with the entity. From the beginning of time this entity has existed whom we now call "Andrew." And how long will this entity called

"Andrew" continue to exist? We think we see the whole movie when in fact we are but looking at just one picture, one snapshot.

So then, you resign out of wisdom. "I don't know what relationship is." Once you have resigned in that way, I wonder what it would be like? I wonder what kind of discord would still be there? But we don't see relationship in this broad sense. We only know identification with the personality. And that is not relationship.

It is very difficult to know true relationship because it is of another level, another dimension. At the level of relationship as we know it, you may side with the child. Your frustration in wanting things to be different, your irritation, comes into it for whatever reason. It could come because you feel the child has to be protected. Or it could also be that the child has brought about disharmony between both parents: "My wife is giving too much attention to the son and I don't get enough." And now we are trying to avoid this approach.

One has to be very, very careful. Unless one resigns one would create the friction. One would create unhappiness in oneself. You cannot take sides. You have to accept the situation as it is.

There is no wisdom in our lives because our relationships are limited to wife, husband, and son — not to Life overall. So what you "think" is right turns out to be wrong. And it makes three people miserable. The minute one personalizes life, there is friction. There would be very few divorces if we could see it that way. But where is the wisdom that has a long-range view? Where is that kind of counsel in today's world that takes relationship out of personality and presents it in this broader view? That wisdom doesn't exist.

The parents may have two different temperaments but that is no justification for destroying the life of the child. The very fact of seeing this would make a difference. It brings sanity into being.

So, learn to resign in this broad, profound way that is beyond the thinking process and perhaps something else would happen.

Question: One wants to try to correct the situation outside of oneself.

I think that is so ninety-nine percent of the time. But we don't know inner correction either. The outer correction doesn't work and we don't know the inner correction. Inner correction is that *you* have to outgrow. You have to see that there are other forces at work.

> *Question:* I see that the only thing I can do is come to my own inner correction, my own rightness. And then if there is anything at all to happen by being resigned, it will be the Divine Forces that will take care of whatever is supposed to happen.

Yes, but what we call "resign" ends up being "indifference." The brain does not know to resign. Anything that is true is not so easy to apply. It's not an adjustment of behavior or mood. There are just as many consequences if we do that kind of resigning. And in the end one begins to feel, "I don't know what to do!"

There might be such a thing as order in the universe. And there might be such a thing as "karma."* There might be a very good reason why a man marries a particular woman and why they give birth to a particular child. It may very

---

* "The law that governs all action and its inevitable consequences on the doer." From *The Ramayana* by C. Rajagopalachari (Bharatiya Vidya Bhavan, Bombay, 1951), page 317.

well be part of the order of the universe rather than that of "you and me."

And it is to this that one resigns. But one can only resign when one has Divine Intelligence. You work with WHAT IS. We want to make WHAT IS into an event. But in actuality the event is your *life span* in this existence as Andrew, Bob, or Betty. And I say that's just an incident in a broad vastness.

If we could understand this we would be very responsible not to get involved in anything. But because we are not responsible, our physical senses, our need for sensation, our need for companionship, our need for this and that personalizes life and the consequences continue. We do not let the Will of God be part of our life. And then when we can't do anything, we say, "I leave it to the Will of God" — as if the brain knows what *that* is.

So there is not much one can do. The child is as subject to those karmic laws as anybody else. If he is to have parents who go in two different directions, he is responsible also. To protect only the child will but increase the tension. The wisdom lies in going beyond this thinking process for it does not know reality.

In India they say, "This happens because in your past life that happened." Somewhere we have many, many debts to pay. We cannot evade it. Mr. J. Krishnamurti has said, "Life is a great responsibility." The only way out is through enlightenment, liberation, salvation.

> *Question:* If I can come to self-correction, would that not provide? Maybe that's the relationship that would extend to my wife and child. I mean, if I could come — not just as an idea — but really come to my own total correction to allow something else to happen, then maybe with that something would change?

Listen to the wisdom of ancient India. They say that if one person becomes enlightened or liberated — one person — then the whole family receives the virtue and the merit of it. All blood relationships become affected. It's so vast. Can you imagine that? It would affect the lives of your children better than anything you could personally do. You cannot put salvation in the second place. You cannot.

So then, if you could leave your child alone and leave your wife alone, and bring about the correction within yourself, you would probably do greater good than wanting to do good for the child.

We're getting down to the core of the issue now. If you do things just for your child, it is going to create friction and you'll get too preoccupied with it. It is better that you come to your own correction and step out of the relative level. Then you will know what to do with your child and your wife. Getting concerned with the child won't work. It'll make things worse.

Question: Is it just another excuse, another delay?

Yes. It may make things worse. You won't be happy. And somebody will ask you, "Why did you get so attached to the boy?" And you will say, "Well, the brain always finds distractions."

Find out who you are attached to. Children are very dangerous, so to speak, because they are so adorable. One gets captivated by them. They are so innocent. Their vulnerability melts one's heart. Well, watch out. Watch out for the little child who is so beautiful and adorable.

You can still be a father, and a better father, you see? You can be a father and a husband at the same time. But don't let either the wife or the child stand in the way.

A long, long time ago people used to worship the sun and the moon. This was around the time of Abraham. And Abraham wondered if there might perhaps be some other force, some other reality behind the sun and the moon that created both of them. It was like the first thought of the One God. So he sat in meditation with a tremendous burning from within to know. And he stuck to it.

Before him came a whirling vortex of energy that took shape. A shining being manifested itself and said, "You want to know what is beyond the sun and the moon?" "Yes," said Abraham. "Then you have to love Him *above all else*." And Abraham promised he would. So then, Isaac was born and slowly, slowly, Abraham became very fond of the child. And the Voice said to him, "You promised to love Him above all else." You know the rest of the story.

Similarly, this is what is meant by resigning to everything. You only resign to everything when God has become your first love. Then everything gets set right. That's the issue. The issue is not your wife; the issue is not your child. They have nothing to do with it. They have their own karma, their own destiny. You cannot improve upon it. It would be a shared indulgence. You cannot personalize life.

Question: No excuses.

No excuses for postponing the only action that each person has to take. Then everything gets corrected. We need to know this, otherwise nothing will work. Unless God is your first love, nothing will work. What has the child to do with it? Better get your own life in order. And the Divine Intelligence is there to help.

So, I am not saying not to love the child but you'll do it better when you have understood what the real purpose of life is. Your relationship with your Creator *must* be your first concern. You cannot give your energy to that by neglecting one relationship or being attached to another. It requires being objective. When you are objective, you will not fuss about why your wife is this way and your child is that way. Even if you try to make outer changes in the family situation, there is no guarantee there will be any better situation elsewhere.

Try to establish some rhythm in your own life. That will have more effect on your child. Bring some kind of order in your own life. It's not an easy thing but this is the clearest way I can point it out. Life is not personality. Life is independent of personality. Therefore let's not get caught and too involved with personality issues.

Take responsibility to do whatever you can do. Whether you like the others or you dislike them, it should not concern you. You act from a totally impersonal way because you have understood relationship. Can you live in the world and be warm and caring for people, but somehow still be with impersonal life? Impersonal life — only then can there be friendship. Otherwise we become dependent and sorrow results. Impersonal life has the right foundation.

Salvation is man's happiest purpose.
Stay with the happiest purpose.

Chapter Two
Healing Relationships

Question: One of the major concepts of *A Course In Miracles* is the healing or correcting of relationship. How does one really heal the relationships that we find ourselves involved in?[1]

We should first define the word relationship so that we are talking about the same thing. Many times we don't really know what a word *means* and therefore we interpret it according to what we *think* it is. But as we become focused or precise in defining what relationship is, most of the confusion, concepts, beliefs, and interpretations are outgrown.

Very few people know what relationship is. What we know — what we call relationship — is dependence. If there is some gratification or something I am gaining from another person, then I think that's a good relationship. And if I cannot mold your opinion according to mine, or you can't mold me according to your likings, then it becomes a bad relationship. But real relationship is not affected by one person's agreeing or disagreeing with another.

Relationship has no opposite to it. It has nothing to do with right or wrong. Relationship is a space beyond likes and dislikes, beyond good and bad, where everything is reconciled and seen in a new light. Do you see? Relationship is not subject to duality. Neither is truth subject to duality. In relationship there is no conflict.

But what we call relationship could be fine now and be a conflict later; it could be loving now and it could be hateful tomorrow. There is no stability in it. Then one is regulated by something external. But what is true is not subject to moods.

So, when we define relationship we find the truth of what relationship *is*. We can see that relationship is independent of personality, like truth and love are independent of personality. If you can love something today and hate it tomorrow then obviously it's not love or relationship. Are we seeing this? That love is not love if it can be turned to hate?

Question: When I initially asked the question I was talking about relationship between you and me.

But where there is another, there is not relationship.

Then you might ask where one finds an example of what relationship is? When Jesus said, "Forgive them for they know not what they do,"[2] He was related with that which does not change, not subject to moods, not regulated from the external. We could say that He had a relationship with what is eternal, what is of God, of truth, of love.

Question: So you are saying that if it is a real relationship that I have with you then it's not regulated in any way by who you are, how you act, or what you do.

If it is regulated then you have some vested interest in some idea, and you are going to try to conform me.

Relationship exists only when you have understood and realized that there is only one life, one God, one truth, one love. Once you've realized that then you see within one life, within

one God, there is relationship with everything.
The tree is related to water. The tree is related to
the soil. The tree is related to the sun. You can't
separate them. Neither can you be separated
from another person or from the carpenter who
made this chair.

So everything is one and within the one there
is a relationship. If we understood that, then we
would probably know what love is. Love would
know what relationship is, for they are both the
same.

> *Question:* What does *A Course In
> Miracles* mean when it talks about
> healing a relationship?

We must realize that whenever I'm condemn-
ing another, whenever I'm blaming and
accusing someone, it is a distortion in my own
mind — some impurity within me. I have to find
out what fear, what motivation there is in me —
what little knowing there is in me that gets
offended. The Course emphasizes:

> *I can be hurt by nothing but my thoughts.*[3]

So, instead of correcting another, how about
correcting it within oneself?

Question: Are you saying that any offense or judgment that I have in relation to another person, no matter what they've done, somehow originates in me?

That's what Christianity is based on. You may say it's not practical or expedient, but you are talking about your helplessness. Then forget about Jesus. He set the example. And so did His apostles. With the exception of one or two they were all martyred. These are men who lived and stood for something — that never deviated because somebody else did something they thought wasn't right.

So, before we set out to heal our relationships, we must know what relationship is. If you know what relationship is then the healing has taken place in you and your perception of your brother has changed, hasn't it? You give him the space; you let him be. And who knows what your peace or the light that would surround you — who knows what impact they would have?

Question: Just the sense of approaching these relationships, or issues, from the standpoint that somewhere the solution or the cause is in myself . . .

The wise always starts with himself. How can you change the other person when you can't even change yourself? The wise person never accuses other people. Whether it's nations or individuals, when they start blaming and accusing others, they are creating fear; they're speaking of the fear in themselves. And they start the armament race.

> *Question:* Other than talking about, or introducing us to this awareness of what relationship is, what else is there in *A Course In Miracles* that helps to bring about this healing?

Well, there is truth in *A Course In Miracles* — just as there is truth in the Bible, in the Koran, and the other scriptures. The issue is, are we going to heed it or are we just going to intellectualize? Who has ". . . the ears to hear?"[4]

I would say that if you have realized your need to heal your relationships, then leave aside abstract ideas about other people. Start with yourself. Ask, "Are there people that I cannot forgive or that I hold grievances against? Are there people I think have done me wrong or that I have some bitterness towards?" I would say that one should find within himself the peace or the space of forgiveness for these people. And if you can come to it then you'll have more peace, won't you? But can *you* bring your relationships to peace? Otherwise they are not relationships, they're dependencies.

In truth, justifications are not valid. People who don't want to get to a profound level explain everything away — build a case against people to justify their holding grievances against them.

For example, can you see if your relationship with your parents is right or do you think they caused every mistake you make? "When I was a child, they did this." And then the psychiatrist comes and says, "Well sure. You are doing wrong things because when you were a child they tied your shoelaces too tight and that's why you hate shoe stores."

> *Question:* One of the things in the Old Testament, as well as in other scriptures, says, "Honour thy father and thy mother."[5] Yet there is so much separation and division now.

There is hardly a family left. Life is getting more and more externalized. "I do as I please..." means that we can live without being responsible. It's a culture that flourishes because it doesn't make a demand. It's the easier side of the easy. And then something degenerates. Ethics, virtue, love for truth, finding out what relationship is — these require wisdom. Learning skills to get a job does not. Where is wisdom today?

But let's come back to the individual and what he can do to heal his relationships. We have some idea that relationship itself is something very holy because we know it is of life itself and no one is separated in it. You and I cannot exist without the light of the sun or the breath of the air. And we did not create them. Neither did the Kremlin nor the Pentagon. The streams flow, the birds fly, and there is dawn. These are of eternal action. Can you relate with that which is eternal, that which is not of man's projection?

It's not only you who have grievances against another, there are nations that have grievances against other nations. Nobody knew one single Vietnamese and yet we could go and drop tons of bombs on them. Without knowing one single person in Afghanistan, you can go and destroy villages and so forth. And it's all justified.

So, I would suggest that one should sit quietly and see, "As long as I have bitterness or hate in me, *I* am not at peace." That's having right relationship with yourself, isn't it? And then you might love being quiet or having some space — becoming less dependent, less distracted. Then begin to see that these are the people you blame and come to some reconciliation within yourself. Find the peace of forgiveness.

A Course In Miracles is based on forgiveness:

> *Forgiveness is the healing of the perception of separation. Correct perception of your brother is necessary, because minds have chosen to see themselves as separate.*[6]

Why should you forgive? For one simple reason. What happened is in the past; it's gone. And you are keeping it alive in the present. Who would call you wise? Even if you did something to me and I did something to you, it's gone and dead. As long as I keep the past alive I'm not alive to the present moment. Therefore, the correction has to take place in me. And once I have corrected that, I would look at you differently. You might have changed. Do you see? Not to forgive is to violate the law that no change takes place. But the creation of God is always creating and changing.

> *Question:* What you are saying is that it's me that carries around the pain,

anxiety, or tension by not letting go of the grievance.

There is something extraordinary in the Bible:

"Therefore if thou bring thy gift to the altar, and there rememberest that thy brother had aught against thee; Leave there thy gift before the altar, and go thy way; first be reconciled to thy brother, and then come and offer thy gift."[7]

There is an urgency about our coming to peace. And we will not come to peace until we have learned to forgive. It is as important as bread and water.

All over the world, about eighty percent of the industry is based on grievances, hate, fear, and insecurity. And what about loneliness? How much money is spent to entertain loneliness? How much money is spent on bitterness and hate and suspicion and doubt about other people? It is between the Arab and the Jew, between the communist and the capitalist. But like John Kenneth Galbraith, the American economist and professor at Harvard, has said, "In communism man exploits man. In capitalism it's just the opposite." We have these belief systems. Don't you see?

If I am not going to be a judgmental person, I will have to think for myself. But I don't think that we even think. We merely react. To think is to be of a pure energy that is independent of reactions and "knowings" and is alive to this moment, untouched by the past or future.

In the present you are related to the planet, to the earth, to heaven. You are related to everything and to every living creature in the world. It is a different state. It doesn't know division. It is not distorted; it is not fragmented. You are whole. And in that wholeness you look through the eyes of holiness and love. And if someone slapped you on one side of the cheek, you "...turn to him the other also. And if any man ...take away your coat, let him have thy cloak also."[8] We are talking about *that* state. And if you compromise, there is just a lot of intellectuality.

To bring forgiveness into application you have to make changes within yourself. Healing your relationships is like stepping out of reactions. You outgrow things and develop a sense of discrimination about what is essential and what is not essential. It is important that you and

I have right relationship — with man, with nature, with God.

I would say that one should take on ten names to start with — people who you think have hurt or wronged you — and really try to come to peace with each person. Find the love and the wisdom in you to forgive. Liberate yourself from your own opinions and the purity of it would transform your life.

The Course makes it clear:

Forgiveness is the key to happiness.[9]

Forgiveness offers everything I want.[10]

What a life that has no blaming or accusation in it! That person is at peace. He has something to give and what he gives would be joyous. He is not afraid of loss and gain. He sees you the way God created you, not the way that you made yourself. We are shaped by society but he would see you as a child of God and not as a citizen of a country, subject to manmade rules.

So, take the ten names and find out that it is just your opinion. Also, that it is gone. Why hoard something that is no longer applicable? You can't recall yesterday's meal when you are hungry today. You need a fresh meal, don't you? All right. So come to the freshness of this moment. Keep this moment impeccable. We have to learn what forgiveness is.

> *Question:* We seem to carry so much from the past into all of the relationships that we come up against.

Yes. And if we do slip and think so and so is this way and so and so is that way, we can find some peace within and say, "It may not be that way. I can't trust my judgment." Then you have to find out what it is that you *can* trust.

You will find that you can trust that which has no opposite — what is profound, not manmade, what is eternal and does not change. You grow in wisdom and you then have something to give to all mankind. You have learned true forgiveness requires that you first heal your relationships with everyone. Then your life has simplicity and you are not so dependent. Your sleep is sleep and your work becomes intrinsic. When your relationship with another person has something divine in it you are not blinded by what you want. You live by some moral ethics, some principles.

Question: What you're saying doesn't make me dependent on someone else. It makes it very clear that I have to do it myself. This is quite a gift.

Learning and understanding are of little value. We fool ourselves. To bring what one has learned and what one knows into *application* is what I am talking about. We already know more than enough. For thousands of years we have known "Thou shalt not kill."[11] Who brings it into application?

I am not deceived by mere learning and having a lot of abstract knowledge. It has no meaning. It has not helped mankind. What helps mankind is the person who brings it into application — lives it. "LOVE YE ONE ANOTHER."[12] *That* being is transformed, not the one who talks about loving and doesn't know what it is.

Chapter Three
All Relationships Must End In Love

---

*B*eing students of *A Course In Miracles* requires that we bring the Course to application. And to do this it would be helpful to know certain laws, certain principles. As far as I'm concerned you are already students of the Course. I will give honesty to that fact. Whether you heed, whether you want to learn, or you don't want to learn, that is your responsibility. I have mine.

It is a joyous thing to have a function. Without it man is lost. There is nothing more meaningful than to know your function, for it brings you into right relationship with everything and everyone.

We do not exist except in relationship. This is a law. It is subject neither to my opinion nor to yours. It is so. We need to learn what relationship is, and we need to bring about a transformation in our relationships with one another.

Perhaps it is because we want to do what we like and follow our own inclinations that we remain ignorant of what relationships *really* are and what responsibility is inherent in them. What lessons are to be learned in relationship? There is no need to mystify the situation; we can deal with it factually.

A Course In Miracles points out that some relationships are but brief encounters, others are more sustained; and still others are lifelong.[1] Have you ever wondered what those relationships might be? Do you see the importance of knowing what relationships are and how to come to right relationship?

In rightness there is freedom. Within right relationship there is freedom also. You try to avoid a particular relationship when you are reacting to it. When you become attached in a relationship, that's not right either. Both have consequences. We see that all too easily. And now we need to deal with these things that are basic, that are right before us — not as philosophy and all kinds of hullabaloo but the actuality of it.

The actuality is that everything has significance — whether it is a relationship with someone we live with or someone we meet at the gas station. According to the Course there are no chance encounters.[2] Pay heed. You must pay heed because you are responsible for how you respond, how you react, what you do or you don't do. Life is a tremendous responsibility. You cannot live at a sub-level, limited to what you like and what you don't like, and pretend you don't know what's going on. It's not enough.

The physical plane is perhaps the only plane we are aware of. This is neither good nor bad. It's just a fact. It is the plane of two forces: cause and effect. What we call science is mostly based on the world of cause and effect. It determines: this is the cause and this is the effect of it. Yet there is further and further one can go. Motivation is very important in the world of cause and effect. To discover what our motivations are is of utmost importance. Since our motivations are of insecurity for the most part, we think the Russians are going to take over, or the Arabs are going to be in control, or whatever. And, as a result, we produce a monstrous society with its violence and weapons.

We need to do something about our motivations — just as we need to understand cause and effect — in order to bring the mind to a state where it is willing to empty itself and,

. . . accept our true relationship with You [God].[3]

Those emptied of mind have the space, the energy, and the wisdom to receive and to accept. *Help us to accept our true relationship with You.* They are not crowded with projections and illusions, nor are they caught in the chaos of the level of motives.

At the level of cause and effect there is very little love in the world. Our relationship is not right with anything. You could be a dentist or a lawyer, a doctor, or whatever, but that position is still secondary to *how* you relate as a doctor, as a lawyer, as an engineer. How we relate is what needs some cleaning up.

We come back again to what *A Course In Miracles* states, that no encounter takes place by accident. So then, what about your family with whom you have a long-range relationship? What about your mother, your father? What about your husband, your wife, your children? Not one of these exists at random or by accident. In each one of these relationships — with family, with aunts, uncles, everyone — correction is needed. There is a healing that is needed, a compassion and understanding that are necessary. And thank the Lord that it is so because now you can grow into being responsible. You know where to begin. You will never know the Peace of God until you do. Isn't that nice? When you don't have the Peace of God, you will have wars outside too. And they are getting more and more dangerous. The world has gone berserk. It is the individual who can change; society never has, never will. But the individual can.

We have to bring right relationship within the family. Are we seeing that? *A Course In Miracles* states that in each encounter there is the potential to learn.[4] If that is understood then we need to question: What is a family? How did families come into being? What are the laws involved? Can you see beauty in why things are the way they are? Can you see the wisdom of creation in it? Have you ever thought about it that way — beyond your opinion?

We need to first see that cause and effect is what has brought the family together: I owe you a debt, you owe me some debt. These are the factors that bring us together. And then, because we have more encounters within the family from childhood, we form strong opinions about "my sister, my father, my brother." In this country just about everyone hates his mother or his father. Goodness gracious. There is very little reverence to be found.

I met a young lady in Carmel, California, when I was coming out of a three-year period of silent retreat. I asked her, "Do you have any friends?" She said her mother was her best friend. I nearly dropped. "Is that so?" "Yes. My mother is my best friend." I was so happy that here was someone who had reverence for her mother.

I asked her where she lived and she took me to her home. As soon as we walked in her mother said, "I want to know the truth. Did you or did you not leave the freezer door open? Now tell me the truth. Speak up." I never saw a more tyrannical mother. The poor girl was embarrassed and in tears.

She wanted to show me the house. Her room had a peace sign on the door and was crowded with feathers and leaves and shells. And then she closed the door because she wanted peace — from "her best friend."

You see, you have to learn how to observe. It is not the eyes that see; it is awareness that sees. If you see only with the eyes you will become judgmental.

Even when you think you love your mother, it may not be true. But let's see if we can make it true by first understanding a principle — I mean *really* understanding. Understanding is more than verbal. We begin by seeing the principle that some divine force has brought the family together. It's not by accident that you married the man or the woman you did; it's not by accident that you have the parents you do. And now, you can bring more love between you and whoever else has been brought into the family with you.

We are talking about a love that is very different, a love that's intelligent, not a dead love. If you have understood what I am talking about, you will take responsibility to come to peace and to harmony with your family.

Let's start undoing. Let's start forgiving. Let's start taking a step out of judgment. The fact is you are part of a family. And now you can love each one. In so doing you will grow centuries. You will be very grateful for each one who is in the family. The family has been put together and each one has a special ability: to push the right button in you. If you are prone to reacting more, then you will probably have a bigger family so that more of your buttons can be pushed.

If you have an opinion about the other, quickly come to forgiveness. What right does anyone have to hold an opinion about another? Your opinion would want the other to conform to your point of view, wouldn't it? Parents succeed in conforming the children, but then the parents get old and the children make them conform. It's "dominate and be dominated." That's not relationship. In right relationship no one dominates another. This we have to learn.

So then, what do we do in relationship? How do we become free from the entanglements, from the involvements? How do we become free of family situations?

Transformation is transformation *in* relationship. If you want to get out of the bind of involvements, you have to bring all relationships to love. That's the only freedom. It's not that you are going to close your eyes and get transformed. You have to bring harmony to everyone you are related to. And in bringing that harmony you grow in wisdom.

Is it not logical, then, that we start with the family? The one you are closest to is probably the one you will be more in conflict with — unless, of course, you like to dominate or be dominated, in which case you destroy one another. Let's see if we can change that.

In the family we have some of the lessons we need to learn right there. No need to read books; it's right before us. But we must see that we are no longer entitled to opinions because it is the very opinions that have brought the lessons about. The opinions are what block the vision of who the other person is.

If we limit life only to opinion — which we do — then there is no forgiveness in it. When your forgiveness is genuine you will see how you can alter opinions. You become energized when you do that. You will see beauty in another that you never saw before because you have put away your resentment and all your "knowings" of yesterday. Why do you want to rubber stamp each day of your life? Make it different, make it new. The sun rises each day; why can't you and I come to new light?

There is a responsibility in being a husband or a wife. It is possible for both to look in the same direction. That's what marriage means. And the direction is what? The direction is that the wife is not looking at the husband and the husband is not looking at the wife — both are looking towards God, towards virtue and ethics, towards a noble way of life. Then both can be a strength to one another. As long as we only look at one another there is going to be a lot of friction, opinion, and judgment. Start changing the direction. Start by changing your own. Don't expect the other to do it. Start with yourself.*

So, have we learned another principle? We began with the fact that we exist in relationship. We learned that the family, where we have closer relationships, is where we can start. And now we have learned another, wonderful principle: you start with yourself. It is no longer abstract. The wise starts with himself, herself. If you start with another, you are going to start with blame. Start with yourself and give the other the space. If the other person doesn't want to change, that's his relationship with God. Just because he has chosen to stay stuck in the quicksand doesn't mean you have to. In the end we are related only to the Source. You are responsible for your own relationship with God.

If you're married and there are clashes, then recognize the wonderful opportunity that is presented. The clashes are what will teach you how to cope with them. If you want a harmonious marriage, then *you* be in harmony. Once you are in harmony, you're out of it.

---

* For a detailed discussion of the issues involved in marital relationships, see *How To Raise A Child Of God* by Tara Singh (Life Action Press, 1987), pages 65-92. (Editor)

I'd like to make one other point. You are responsible for looking after your parents as long as they are alive. Whether they are good or bad according to your point of view, you must still have reverence for your parents. You cannot dump them on the mercy of televisions and old people's homes.

So, begin where you are and you will have a handful. Aren't you glad you have families?

All relationships must end in love. In love there is no cause and effect. You move from reactions and the "knowings" of the physical senses to something that goes beyond — to thoughtfulness, consideration, and love. You keep evolving that way till the whole of mankind becomes your family.

We are not trying to get rid of families. We are trying to lead you to a greater family — that of all mankind on earth. If you get defeated by the little family you are in — well, what are you going to do? Now don't tell me you don't have homework to do. The instruction has been given.

There is another aspect of relationship we need to deal with. Let's say I am in disagreement with you and then we both part for four or five years. I have forgotten you and you have forgotten me and we think everything is all right. That's the way of life, especially in this part of the world: leave one relationship and go start another one and another one. Hardly anyone has a family and therefore we get into more and more involvements. But the original involvements may not be over. Those relationships you thought you were done with (you know, you got rid of them and now you're preoccupied with this new one), well, they are going to pop up in one form or another because those lessons still need to be learned.

As *A Course In Miracles* explains:

> . . . *the second level of teaching is a more sustained relationship, in which, for a time, two people enter into a fairly intense teaching-learning situation and then appear to separate. . . . these meetings are not accidental, nor is what appears to be the end of the relationship a real end. Again, each has learned the most he can at the time. Yet all who meet will someday meet again, for it is the destiny of all relationships to become holy.*[5]

The Course is saying that if you failed to learn the lessons the first time, you will be given another opportunity to see if you have come to love and are no longer in the bondage of memory or resentment — the poisons you had been carrying. Don't you want to be free of that? What other freedom is there but freedom from your own opinions?

Freed from opinions, you see the fallacy of reaction and the responsibility of coming to love. You will probably even be grateful because the one you most dislike is your best teacher. Don't you want a challenging teacher? Well, there he is. And when you have succeeded no one will have to tell you; you'll know it.

If you have seen the fact that there is no sense in disagreement, you will also give another the space to be who and what he is. You can still care for someone but you won't have conditions any more. And who knows, both may see each other differently.

Your responsibility is to yourself. If you have forgotten the past and are no longer reacting, you are with the new. You have come to new birth, to a new start. Isn't that wonderful? In this lifetime you can end all unfinished relationships. It could be with hundreds of people. Life would bring them around. And you thought it was all over! The unfinished business always pops up.

Your responsibility is to never wish things to be any different than the way they are. If you have come to the level where your opinion about another no longer dominates you, you have become a person who cannot be affected by whatever another person does. You meet the situation with love — real love. That means you are no longer part of the effect. When you are the cause — and the cause is love — you cannot be affected and, for you, that relationship has been completed whether or not it has been for the other.

The first time, perhaps you both reacted or you both had opinions. But by the time the situation comes up a second time, if you are wise, you will have grown in tolerance, in wisdom, in goodness. That would be the natural thing, if you are growing at all. If you have been evolving towards wisdom and maturity, then a meeting takes place in which your thoughtfulness, your wisdom, your love cannot be affected by the external. Then you are not part of an involvement even though the other person could still be. You will look upon another differently without making so many problems. How it "should be" is no longer your concern.

If the other person has not yet wiped out the past he will still hold onto those grudges, even if those particular circumstances no longer exist. He cannot meet you anew. How we hold on to those past grievances! Seldom do we ever meet anyone anew. It is but our memory that we meet again and again. "I know who you are!" How poisonous this is.

Why do you like your "knowing" so much? It is chaotic. Can't you get rid of it? At least before you go to sleep sit quiet and see if you can get away from your "knowings." Better start meditating; to undo the known is its purpose. That is the way to grow if you want to come to love.

Sit quiet in the evening and undo all the events of the day. The brain will automatically bring the events to your attention because one of its functions is to bring order. We have abused the brain; we've not understood it. Now our brain is always confused, always wanting, always hateful. It is crowded with memory — like being jammed in a tar pit. Nothing moves. It has gotten crystallized and fixed. And yet the brain is something so sensitive and alive.

Observe the events of the day. The brain will try to bring to your attention what needs to be attended to. So attend to it. Try to meditate for an hour if possible before you go to bed. At first everything is going to rush into your mind. This may go on for months and months but don't get discouraged by it. Just see how much you must have suppressed, how dull you have been in ignoring it, and now you are paying the price. You have a relationship inside of you too. Let it be, it's all right. Slowly an awareness will come and an awakening will take place. *It* will observe and the brain will not disturb it. This light, this awareness, this sensitivity, this attention will grow in proportion to your understanding of what we have been talking about.

Just observe and do not interpret. You will recognize your opinions about other people are just opinions. Don't interfere. Let it be and it will have less and less power because something in you cannot be affected by it anymore. What a new beginning! Something in you cannot be affected. How beautiful when you come to a point where your opinion about someone no longer affects you. You are becoming mature. It is like the gift of the Grace of God upon you.

The joy and passion in you to end the involvements will grow like wildfire. See it; undo it. Your stillness undoes everything. That is the state of meditation in which there is no separation between anyone, for you no longer have opinions. You value that which is real, that which is still, that which is in harmony with everything that exists. And it is so compassionate that it helps you in what your function is: to bring order in your brain and in your relationships. You assume responsibility for what you do and what you have done. "Know thyself" is the beginning of wisdom.

When you are liberated from reactions and you are no longer affected, you will affect humanity. The innocence and the intensity of your stillness affect mankind upon the earth. Your words have power. And those words never die, for they are not born of time and personality.

Eternal words are the light of the world and they remain accessible to someone else throughout the centuries. Leave behind words that are eternal. Leave behind words that are a light upon the planet. Words that are true and eternal are indivisible. They do not divide anything; they bring things together. We live in a fragmented world of boundaries, names, and forms, of separation and friction. Let your words be those that are indivisible, not subject to time, but eternal. Then you will have lived as a Son of God upon this planet.

Let us see if we can make those corrections. Do it quietly and bring things to gratefulness. Gratefulness liberates man. It purifies the insanity of negativity. Awaken to gratefulness and you will see how sensitive it will make you. The world is full of goodness and your gratefulness would add to it. Learn to be grateful and you will never be involved. To forgive, not to judge, and to be grateful — that is the message of *A Course In Miracles*.

"The Timeless Gifts"

All things that God created timeless are
His gifts to me. The passing and the frail
Are not a part of my inheritance.
Such are His promises. He cannot fail
To keep them perfectly. His sacred Word
Is given me in silence. I will trust
In Him because I listened and I heard.

This poem is from *The Gifts Of God* by the scribe of *A Course In Miracles* (Foundation for Inner Peace, 1982, page 32). It is an incomparable book of poetry containing some of the most important words ever spoken.

Addenda

The Path of Virtue

The purpose of the Foundation for Life Action
is to be with the Eternal Laws
so that it does not become an organization.

LOVE IS ETERNAL.
ABILITIES EXTENDING LOVE ARE BLESSED.

In the absence of Love
abilities become the bondage of skills,
limited to personality.
Among virtuous men,
it is what the human being is that is Real,
and not what he does in a body.

The purpose of the Foundation is to be part of

GOD'S PLAN FOR SALVATION.[1]

Thus it has a different point of reference
than the thought system of man.

"LOVE HOLDS NO GRIEVANCES"

Obviously, the Name of God
cannot be commercialized.
There are no fees in what we share.
We do not believe in loss and gain.
Non-commercialized action is provided by
the blessings of productive life.

"IN GOD WE TRUST"

Those who are with the Eternal Laws
in times of change remain unaffected.
In crisis, it is your care for another
that is your strength.

We have a function in the world
to be truly helpful to others,
knowing:

> *I am sustained by the Love of God.*[2]

> *My only function is the one God gave me.*[3]

> *Nothing real can be threatened.*
> *Nothing unreal exists.*[4]

We are not pressured
by the brutality of success.
We are blessed by the work we do.
Gratefulness is complete,
as love is independent.

To us, you, the human being, come first.
Thus it enables us to go past
the conventional opinion of right and wrong
and relate directly to you.

For man is as God created him,
unchanged by the changeable society
that rules his body with its belief systems.

The Truth is a Fact that dissolves
illusions of time.
Our function is to dispel
the abstraction of ideas
and realize the actuality of Fact.

For,

> *I am under no laws but God's.*[5]

Reverence for Life is of a still mind
hallowed by His Love.
This transformation is what we call

THE PATH OF VIRTUE.

The Path of Virtue
is the ministry of gratefulness.

The wise who extends
the Kingdom of God on earth
lives consistent with

"BUT SEEK YE FIRST THE KINGDOM OF GOD,
AND HIS RIGHTEOUSNESS;
AND ALL THINGS
SHALL BE ADDED UNTO YOU."[6]

Biography of Tara Singh

*T*ara Singh is known as a teacher, author, poet, and humanitarian. The early years of his life were spent in a small village in Punjab, India. From this sheltered environment his family then traveled and lived in Europe and Central America. At twenty-two, his search for Truth led him to the Himalayas where he lived for four years as an ascetic. During this period he outgrew conventional religion and discovered that a mind conditioned by religious or secular beliefs is always limited.

In his next phase of growth he responded to the poverty of India through participation in that country's postwar industrialization and international affairs. He became a close friend of Prime Minister Nehru as well as Eleanor Roosevelt.

It was in the 1950's, as he outgrew his involvement with political and economic systems, that Mr. Singh was inspired by his association with Mr. J. Krishnamurti and the teacher of the

Dalai Lama. He discovered that mankind's problems cannot be solved externally. Subsequently, he became more and more removed from worldly affairs and devoted several years of his life to the study and practice of yoga. The discipline imparted through yoga helped make possible a three year period of silent retreat in Carmel, California, in the early 1970's.

As he emerged from the years of silence in 1976, he came into contact with *A Course In Miracles*. Its impact on him was profound. He recognized its unique contribution as a scripture and saw it as the answer to man's urgent need for direct contact with Truth. There followed a close relationship with the Scribe of *A Course In Miracles*. The Course has been the focal point of his life ever since.

Mr. Singh's love of the Course has inspired him to share it in workshops and retreats throughout the United States. He recognizes and presents the Course as Thoughts of God and correlates it with the great spiritual teachings and religions of the world. From Easter 1983 to Easter 1984, Mr. Singh conducted the One Year Non-Commercialized Retreat: A Serious Study of *A Course In Miracles*. It was an unprecedented, in-depth exploration of the Course. No tuition was charged.

Mr. Singh continues to work closely with serious students of the Course under the sponsorship of the Foundation for Life Action, a school for bringing *A Course In Miracles* into application and for training teachers of *A Course In Miracles*. He is the author of numerous books and has been featured on many audio and videotapes in which he discusses the action of bringing one's life into order, freeing oneself from past conditioning, and living the principles of the Course. He offers two regularly scheduled retreats on *A Course In Miracles* annually: New Year's and Easter.

References

PREFACE TO THE THIRD EDITION
1. *A Course In Miracles* (ACIM), *Workbook For Students* (II), page 114. *A Course In Miracles*, first published in 1976 by the Foundation for Inner Peace, Tiburon, California, is a contemporary scripture which deals with the psychological/spiritual issues facing man today. It consists of three volumes: *Text* (I), *Workbook For Students* (II), and *Manual For Teachers* (III). The *Text*, 622 pages, sets forth the concepts on which the thought system of the Course is based. The *Workbook For Students*, 478 pages, is designed to make possible the application of the concepts presented in the *Text* and consists of three hundred and sixty-five lessons, one for each day of the year. The *Manual For Teachers*, 88 pages, provides answers to some of the basic questions a student of the Course might ask and defines many of the terms used in the *Text*. (Editor)
2. Refers to Lession 47 of *A Course In Miracles*, *"God is the Strength in which I trust."*
3. ACIM, II, page 116.

INTRODUCTION
1. ACIM, II, page 143.
2. ACIM, II, page 114.

PART I

CHAPTER ONE: CLEAR DIRECTION

1. ACIM, II, page 114.
2. ACIM, I, page 51.
3. ACIM, I, page 49.
4. ACIM, I, page 24.
5. ACIM, II, page 114.
6. ACIM, II, page 115.
7. Ibid.

CHAPTER THREE: THE ENDING OF ATTACK

1. ACIM, II, page 116.
2. Ibid.
3. Ibid.
4. Ibid.
5. ACIM, I, page 6.
6. ACIM, II, page 116.
7. Ibid.
8. Ibid.
9. Ibid.
10. Ibid.
11. ACIM, II, pages 116-117.
12. ACIM, II, page 119.
13. ACIM, II, page 117.
14. Ibid.
15. Ibid.

PART II

CHAPTER TWO: HEALING RELATIONSHIPS

1. *"Healing Relationships"* is an adaptation of an interview conducted by Charles Johnson, Co-Director of the Foundation for Life Action, which has been broadcast as a part of the

Exploring A Course In Miracles radio and television series. (Editor)
2. Luke 23:34.
3. ACIM, II, page 428.
4. Matthew 11:15.
5. Exodus 20:12.
6. ACIM, I, page 41.
7. Matthew 5:23-24.
8. Matthew 5:39-40.
9. ACIM, II, page 210.
10. ACIM, II, page 213.
11. Exodus 20:13.
12. John 13:34.

CHAPTER THREE:
ALL RELATIONSHIPS MUST END IN LOVE
1. See ACIM, III, page 7.
2. See ACIM, III, page 6.
3. This is a line from the prayer which appears in the *Text* of *A Course In Miracles*, page 326: *Forgive us our illusions, Father, and help us to accept our true relationship with You, in which there are no illusions, and where none can ever enter. Our holiness is Yours. What can there be in us that needs forgiveness when Yours is perfect? The sleep of forgetfulness is only the unwillingness to remember Your forgiveness and Your Love. Let us not wander into temptation, for the temptation of the Son of God is not Your Will. And let us receive only what You have given, and accept but this into the minds which You created and which You love. Amen.* This prayer has been referred to as *A Course In Miracles'* version of the Lord's Prayer. See *Journey Without Distance: The Story Behind A Course In Miracles* by Robert Skutch

(Celestial Arts, 1984), page 68. The prayer is discussed in great detail in *Dialogues On A Course In Miracles* by Tara Singh (Life Action Press, 1987), pages 35-167. (Editor)
4. See ACIM, III, pages 6-7.
5. ACIM, III, page 7.

ADDENDA: THE PATH OF VIRTUE
1. ACIM, II, page 120.
2. ACIM, II, page 79.
3. ACIM, II, page 107.
4. ACIM, I, Introduction.
5. ACIM, II, page 132.
6. Matthew 6:33

Other Materials by Tara Singh
Related to A Course In Miracles

BOOKS

How To Learn From A Course In Miracles
A Course In Miracles — A Gift For All Mankind
Commentaries On A Course In Miracles
The Voice That Precedes Thought
Dialogues On A Course In Miracles
The Future Of Mankind — The Branching Of The Road
How To Raise A Child Of God
"Nothing Real Can Be Threatened" (forthcoming)

AUDIO CASSETTE TAPES

A Course In Miracles Explorations
The Heart Of Forgiveness
Discussions On A Course In Miracles
"What Is The Christ?"
Freedom From Belief
Discovering Your Own Holiness
Finding Peace Within
Discovering Your Life's Work
What Is A Course In Miracles?
How To End The Sorrow Of Man
"Creation's Gentleness Is All I See"
Living With Integrity

Psychological Pressures:
    What They Are And How To Deal With Them
All Relationships Must End In Love
To Know Truth Beyond Words
A Life Of Non-Compromise
"My Only Function Is The One God Gave Me"
You Are The Altar Of God
Trust Versus Belief
The Gift Of Remembrance
Prayer And Forgiveness
Begin With Gratefulness
"Removing The Blocks
    To The Awareness Of Love's Presence"
Wisdom Begins With Self-Knowing
What Are You Going To Give This World?
"I Want The Peace Of God"
Undoing Self-Deception
"This You Will Never Teach"
"As I Have Loved You"
Tara Singh Tapes from the One Year
    Non-Commercialized Retreat: A Serious
    Study of A Course In Miracles

BOOKS ON AUDIO CASSETTE TAPE

How To Learn From A Course In Miracles
Commentaries On A Course In Miracles (selections)
Transforming Your Marriage
    (Chapter Three from *How To Raise A Child Of God*)
The Voice That Precedes Thought (selections)
How To Raise A Child Of God (selections)
"Love Holds No Grievances" (selections)

VIDEO CASSETTE TAPES

A Course In Miracles And The Destiny Of America
I Would Be Lost Without A Course In Miracles
"I Have A Function God Would Have Me Fill"
"Give Me Your Blessing, Holy Son Of God"
"Do Only That" —
 A Course In Miracles And Working With Children
The Power Of Attention
A Course In Miracles And The Limitation Of Learning
"If I Defend Myself I Am Attacked"
The Step From Illusion To Truth
The Function Of A Teacher Is To End Deception
"Nothing Real Can Be Threatened" —
 A Workshop On A Course In Miracles
 Part I *— The Question And The Holy Instant*
 Part II *— The Deception Of Learning*
 Part III *— Transcending The Body Senses*
 Part IV *— Awakening To Self Knowledge*
Finding Your Inner Calling
How To Raise A Child Of God
Exploring A Course In Miracles (series)
 — What Is A Course In Miracles?
   and *"The Certain Are Perfectly Calm"*
 — God Does Not Judge and *Healing Relationships*
 — Man's Contemporary Issues
   and *Life Without Consequences*
 — Principles and *Gratefulness*
A Call to Wisdom and
 A Call To Wisdom — Exploring A Course In Miracl
Man's Struggle For Freedom From The Past
 and *"Beyond This World There Is A World I Want"*

Life For Life
        and *Moneymaking Is Inconsistent With Life Forces*
The Call To Wisdom:
        A Discussion On A Course In Miracles (Parts I & II)
"Quest Four" with Damien Simpson
        and Stacie Hunt
"Odyssey" and *"At One With"* with Keith Berwick

**Book and tape catalogues are available from
Life Action Press.**

Additional copies of *"Love Holds No Grievences" – The Ending Of Attack* may be obtained by sending a check, Mastercard or Visa number and expiration date to:

LIFE ACTION PRESS
902 South Burnside Avenue
Los Angeles, CA 90036
213/933-5591

Softcover $5.95
(plus $2.00 shipping/handling)

A Course In Miracles may be purchased from the Foundation for Inner Peace, P.O. Box 1104, Glen Ellen, California 95442. It may also be purchased from Life Action Press:

Three volume, hardbound edition $40.00
(plus $3.00 shipping/handling)
Combined, softcover edition $25.00
(plus $3.00 shipping/handling)

California residents please add 6.5% sales tax.

Thank you.

Design:	Lucille Frappier and Clio Dixon
Composition:	Acacia Williams and Jim Cheatham
Software:	Xerox Desktop Publishing Series:
	Ventura Publisher Edition
Typesetting:	FingerPrint Desktop Publishers,
	Los Angeles, California
Printing/binding:	McNaughton & Gunn, Inc.,
	Saline, Michigan
Typeface:	Palatino
Paper:	55lb Glatfelter natural (acid free)